Peace, Love & Blessings

To My Family & Friends

Thank You For Your Love & Support

ISBN: 1-4392-2158-8
ISBN-13: 9781439221587
Library of Congress Control Number: 2008911563

Visit www.booksurge.com to order additional copies.

About the Book
Empowered children make great decisions to not give up and trust God in the good and bad times. Some make mistakes and have troubles along the way, but they all find encouragement and strength to accomplish their goals.

About the Author
Betty Zikusooka is a devoted wife and mother. She believes that it is important to nurture the ambitions within our children and do away with self-limiting beliefs. She wants all children to know that they are special and amazing.

She writes inspirational literature to plant seeds of faith in the hearts of readers. Her books are established in God's Word and designed to encourage, build character and infuse confidence and wisdom.

Her prayer is for each reader to know God personally through salvation and relationship. She also desires for readers to be strengthen and encouraged to believe enough in their dreams to live them.

About the Illustrator
Gerrie "Crushow" Herring II has loved art since he was a toddler. Crushow is a dedicated father and mentor. He has partnered with others to implement youth art programs and to spread a national youth movement that acts as a bridge between communities in need and the young people who want to help make them better. Crushow has showcased his exceptional talent throughout Los Angeles by painting murals for the YMCA, Boost Mobile, Rock Corps, Media Star Promotions, and others.

Foreword

When faced with adversity we have the option to remain in our disappointment or complete what has been set before us. Dwelling in our dissatisfaction will not change what may have been lost. But accepting God's strength in our weakness will help us to rise above our displeasure. Each new day brings new opportunities.

… My grace is sufficient for thee for my strength
is made perfect in weakness
2 Corinthians 12: 7-9

I can do all things through Christ who strengthen me.

Philippians 4:13

I can finish what I start.

I just take one step at a time.

God gives me what I need to work hard stuff out.

Princess Jewel finished the puzzle.

She added one new piece at a time.

...With God all things are possible.
Matthew 19:26

I am smart.

I can do anything I put my mind to.

But sometimes I get mad
when my work
gives me trouble.

And sometimes I feel sad when my work seems too hard, but I don't let that stop me.

God helps me rise above trouble.

Chelsea Grace finished
her homework.

God is our refuge and strength
an ever-present help in trouble.
Psalm 46:1

I always try my best, but sometimes my best
does not seem good enough.

Sometimes I fall and I
don't feel like getting up.

Jonah 2:7

9

Sometimes I cry.

But after I cry, I wipe away my tears.

John 16:20

God helps me get up
when I fall.

Carmen Strong got up after she fell.
She is now a top skater.

*The Lord upholds all
those who fall.   Psalm 145:14*

The race goes to the one who holds on to the end.

So, I keep going. It does not matter what it looks like.

James 5:11

12

I keep going because I trust God.

C.J. passed two runners and won the race.

We live by faith not by sight.
2 Corinthians 5:7

New things may seem
scary at first.

I may not master some
things the first time.

But my hope is bigger than my fear.

2 Timothy 1:7
and Romans 5:5

God is my helper.

Takia Bell did not give up.
     She learned to ride.
She is now a great bike rider.

*We say with confidence,
the Lord is my helper and I will
not be afraid.   Hebrews 13:6*

Practice is good.

Believing in myself
is excellent.

God says I can because
I am wonderful.

After much practice,
Starr Joy now hula
hoops very well.

I praise you because I am
fearfully and wonderfully made.
Psalm 139:14

GOD SAYS I CAN

I can rise above stuff

I can finish what I start

I am smart

I am strong

I am able

Let's Review

Fill in the blanks using the words in the box.

> all finish faith holds rise get up what
> great wonderful need trust

1. I can do _____ things through Christ who strengthens me.

2. I _____ what I start.

3. God gives me what I _____ to work things out.

4. God helps me to _____ above problems.

5. God helps me to _____ when I fall.

6. I keep going because I _____ God.

7. The race goes to the one who _____ on to the end.

8. We live by _____ not by sight.

9. Believing in myself is _____.

10. I am _____.

GOD'S PROMISES TO YOU

**God promises to come into your heart and forgive you for your sins.
All you have to do is believe in him and ask him.**

Romans 10:9
YOU CAN BE SAVED!

... if you confess with your mouth , "Jesus is Lord," and believe in your heart that God rasied him from the dead, you will be saved.

John 3:16
YOU CAN HAVE ETERNAL LIFE!

For God so loved the world that he gave his one and only son that whoever believe in him shall not perish but have eternal life.

Acts 2:38
YOU CAN HAVE THE HOLY SPIRIT!

...Repent and be baptized, everyone of you in the name of Jesus Christ for the forgiveness of your sins. And you will receive the gift of the Holy Spirit.

YES, JESUS LOVES YOU!
YES, JESUS IS YOUR ANSWER, TRUTH, AND LIGHT!

BIBLE STUDY

Learn more about Jesus and how much he loves you by reading His Word.

1. Find a verse you like in the Bible. 2. Copy it onto a piece of paper.	3. Draw a picture by the verse. 4. Tell someone what the verse means to you.

5. Choose a new verse each day to copy, draw a picture by, and tell someone about.

Great Bible Scriptures to look up and study

John 14   John 15   John 16   John 17

Below are more of my favorite Bible verses=
Be encouraged!

The Lord is my strength and my song; he has become my salvation. He is my God and I will praise him.
Exodus 15:2

Trust in the Lord with all your heart and lean not on your own understanding; in all your ways acknowledge him, and he will make your paths straight.
Proverbs 3:5-6

Daughter, your faith has healed you. Go in peace and be freed from your suffering.
Mark 5:34

Then he said to her, "Daughter, your faith has healed you. Go in peace."
Luke 8:48

Therefore, if anyone is in Christ, he is a new creation; the old has gone, the new has come!
2 Corinthians 5:17

Therefore, since we have been justifed through faith, we have peace with God through our Lord Jesus Christ, through whom we have gained access by faith into his grace in which we stand. And rejoice in the hope of the glory of God.
Romans 5:1-2

In the same way the Spirit helps us in our weakness. We do not know what we ought to pray for, but the Spirit himself intercedes for us with groans that words cannot express.
Romans 8:26

…, in all these things we are more that conquerors through him who loved us.
Romans 8:37

For the foolishness of God is wiser than man's wisdom, and the weakness of God is stronger than mans's strength.
1 Corinthians 1:25

I have hidden your word in my heart that I might not sin against you.
Psalm 119 :11

For it is by grace you have been saved, through faith ---and this is not from yourselves, it is the gift of God.
Ephesians 2:8-9

Brothers, we do not want you to be ignorant about those who fall asleep, or to grieve like ther rest of men, who have no hope. We believe that Jesus died and rose again and so we believe that God will bring with Jesus those who have fallen asleep in him.
1 Thessalonians 4:13-14

Now may the Lord of peace himself give you peace at all time and in every way. The Lord be with all of you.
2 Thessalonians 3:16

So do not throw away your confidence, it will be richly rewarded.
Hebrews 10:35

GOD BLESS YOU!
THANK YOU FOR READING!

Amen

… I am with you always…

    Matthew 28:20

...God is Love...

            1 John 4:8

Scriptures references come from The NIV Study Bible,
10th Anniversary Edition
Published by Zondervan Publishing House, Grand Rapids, MI 49530, USA.

Made in the USA
Charleston, SC
14 January 2010